Stupid

Car

Salesman

Jokes

Stupid Car Salesman Jokes

R.K. REID

ISBN: 9798266897328

Disclaimer

This is a humor and parody book meant for entertainment only.

Stupid Car Salesman Jokes is not affiliated with or endorsed by any organizations or related communities.

The author and publisher take no responsibility for hurt feelings, bruised egos, or sudden awareness of questionable career choices.

Hey Car Sales Pros:
You've been warned…

Stupid Jokes Await !!!

Dedication

To my beloved and ever-entertaining furry friends, Mr. Chai and Maile, this book is dedicated to you both.

Your playful antics and unwavering support have inspired this collection of silly one-liner jokes.

Your mischievous charms & naughty antics will always be remembered.

I always love you guys!

A Message for You

To: _____

From: _____

Date: _____

A note from your gift giver:

_____

_____

_____

_____

_____

*May this book bring you lots
of laughter and brighten your day!*

What Should I Write Here?

This book template seems to have run out of creative juice.

Perhaps I can seize this opportunity to shamelessly promote my website.

Hey there! Take a gander at my marvelous online realm:

www.stupidjokebooks.com

Prepare yourself for an extraordinary experience with my breathtaking selection of "Stupid" joke books.

Caution: Excessive laughter and inevitable disappointment await!

Contents

(Jokes On You!)

(There Are No Page Numbers!)

*"Car salesmen don't lie…
they just practice
extremely optimistic
storytelling."*

Why do car salesmen love calculators more than customers?

Because calculators actually give you the numbers you want to see, unlike credit applications that turn dreams into "Sorry, we need a co-signer."

Fun Fact: The average car salesman performs 47 payment calculations per customer, only to hear "I need to think about it overnight."

There once was a salesman named Pete,
Who lived on coffee and no sleep, He'd
show cars all day, For minimal pay,
While customers promised "next week!"

Fun Fact: *Car salesmen consume 400%*
more caffeine than the general population,
yet still can't stay awake during finance
meetings.

What breaks a car salesman's heart more than a breakup?

Watching a customer you spent three hours with walk across the street to buy the exact same car from your competitor for $200 less.

Fun Fact: *Studies show 73% of car salesmen have trust issues, and 89% of those are directly caused by customers saying "I'll be back tomorrow."*

A customer walked in one day, Said "I'm just looking, if that's okay," Three hours later, Still no buyer, But they know every car's MPG!

Fun Fact: *Professional browsers can inspect 47 vehicles, test drive 12, and remember none of the prices when they finally decide to buy.*

Why do car salesmen become expert mathematicians?

Because they can calculate monthly payments 17 different ways, but somehow customers always want it $50 cheaper than physically possible.

Fun Fact: The phrase "What do I need to do to earn your business today?" has been said 2.4 million times in dealerships this week.

What's the difference between closing time and a customer's decision-making process?

Closing time eventually happens, but customers will "think about it" until the heat death of the universe.

Fun Fact: *Car salesmen have developed supernatural abilities to sense when someone is about to say "We need to sleep on it" from 50 feet away.*

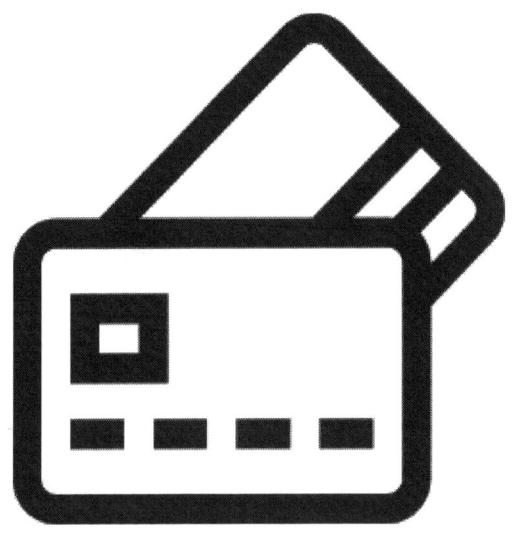

There once was a buyer named Claire, Whose credit was beyond repair, She wanted BMW, With payments of two, The salesman just started to stare.

Fun Fact: *Financing miracles occur daily in dealerships, turning 480 credit scores into "Let me talk to my manager" success stories.*

Why are car salesmen the world's most optimistic people?

Because they genuinely believe that this time, the customer who says "We're definitely buying today" actually means it.

Fun Fact: *The average car salesman experiences 14 emotional breakdowns per month, all triggered by the phrase "Can you do better on the price?"*

What's a car salesman's biggest fear?

Not losing a sale to price, but finding out the customer bought the exact same car from the internet for the same payment three months later.

Fun Fact: *Car salesmen check their competitors' websites more obsessively than teenagers check social media, and with significantly more anxiety.*

A salesman named Bob loved his phone, He'd research trades when left alone, But when customers came, They'd play the same game, "I'll Google it" – then they were gone.

Fun Fact: *Modern car buying involves 73 Google searches, 14 YouTube reviews, and exactly zero phone calls to the dealership for information.*

What's the most prestigious award in car sales?

Salesman of the Month, which you win by selling 12 cars while everyone else sold 11, but you all still can't afford the cars you're selling.

Fun Fact: *The Salesman of the Month parking spot is always empty because the winner is too busy following up with customers who "just need one more day."*

Why do car salesmen carry so many keys?

Because every test drive is potentially "the one," even though 47% end with "Thanks, we'll call you" and immediate radio silence.

Fun Fact: *The average key ring in a dealership weighs 3.7 pounds and contains keys to vehicles that were sold six months ago but never picked up.*

What do car salesmen see when they look in the mirror?

Someone who can sell ice to an eskimo, but somehow can't convince their own mother to buy gap insurance.

Fun Fact: Car salesmen practice their closing techniques on their reflection daily, yet still crack under pressure when asked about the warranty details.

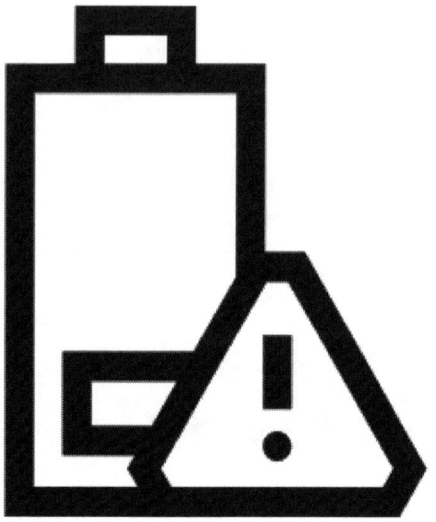

There was a salesman whose energy died, From customers who had to decide, He recharged with hope, But without sale scope, His commission just slowly subsided.

Fun Fact: *Car salesmen's energy levels are directly proportional to the customer's financing approval chances and inversely related to the phrase "just looking."*

Why do car salesmen love pizza delivery guys?

Because they're the only people who understand what it's like to drive around all day hoping someone actually wants what you're bringing them.

Fun Fact: *The dealership break room pizza has witnessed more sales strategy meetings than the actual conference room, and significantly more tears.*

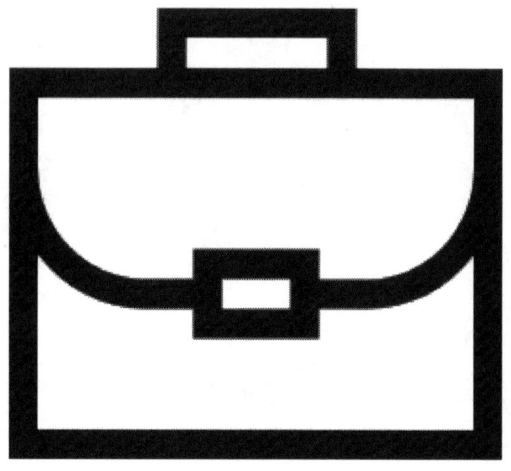

What's in a car salesman's briefcase?

45 business cards, 12 financing calculators, 3 energy drinks, and the crushing weight of unrealistic monthly sales goals.

Fun Fact: *Car salesmen's briefcases contain more broken promises than actual paperwork, mostly in the form of customer contact information that goes straight to voicemail.*

Why are car salesmen terrible at buying houses?

Because they keep trying to negotiate monthly payments instead of purchase price, and they can't stop asking "What do I need to do to earn your business today?"

Fun Fact: *Real estate agents report that car salesmen are their most difficult clients because they instinctively distrust anyone in a sales profession.*

A customer made Jimmy weep, By saying the price was too steep, He dropped it down low, They still said "We'll go," And bought one while Jimmy did sleep.

Fun Fact: *The phrase "We found the same car cheaper down the street" has caused more automotive PTSD than actual car accidents.*

When do car salesmen have their best ideas?

At 3 AM when they remember that customer from Tuesday who said maybe, and suddenly have the perfect closing line that definitely would have worked.

Fun Fact: *Car salesmen experience their most brilliant sales revelations during insomnia, which is caused by thinking about all the sales they almost closed.*

What's a car salesman's relationship with time?

They live in a perpetual state of "end of month panic" while customers exist in "I have all the time in the world to decide" purgatory.

Fun Fact: *The last three days of every month contain 47% of all automotive sales and 73% of all salesman mental breakdowns.*

Why do car salesmen make terrible doctors?

Because their diagnosis for every customer is "acute payment sensitivity" and their only prescription is "have you considered a longer loan term?"

Fun Fact: *Car salesmen can diagnose a customer's credit score within 30 seconds of meeting them, with 87% accuracy based purely on their shoes and phone model.*

There once was a grad with degree, Who thought car sales would be easy, First day on the lot, Reality hit hot, Now "just looking" makes him queasy.

Fun Fact: *Business school never teaches the advanced mathematics required to make a $299/month payment work on a $45,000 car with no money down.*

Why are car salesmen natural performers?

Because they deliver the same "this is the best deal I've ever offered" speech 47 times per week with genuine enthusiasm each time.

Fun Fact: The Academy Awards should have a category for "Best Performance by a Salesman Explaining Why the Extended Warranty is Actually a Great Deal."

What's a car salesman's favorite game?

Darts, because it's the only place where missing the target by six inches doesn't cost you a $400 commission check.

Fun Fact: *Car salesmen have better aim throwing darts after work than they do hitting their monthly sales goals, despite significantly more practice with the latter.*

Why is toilet paper more reliable than car customers?

Because when you need it, it's actually there, unlike customers who promise to come back Saturday and then vanish into the automotive ether.

Fun Fact: *Dealerships go through more tissues (for crying salesmen) than toilet paper, making it a surprisingly accurate business expense predictor.*

A salesman went out for a drink, To forget customers who made him think, But even the wine, Couldn't make it fine, That he'd lost three deals at the brink.

Fun Fact: *Car salesmen consume 340% more alcohol than the national average, yet still can't forget the customer who left to "think about it" in 2019.*

What's the best-selling book among car salesmen?

*"How to Win Friends and Influence People,"
which is ironic because their job is literally
winning friends and influencing people to
buy cars.*

Fun Fact: *The self-help section of
dealership break rooms contains more
books than the local library, yet nobody can
help themselves stop checking trade-in
values.*

Why do car salesmen make terrible fortune tellers?

Because they predict every customer will buy today, but somehow they're always surprised when people say "We need to think about it overnight."

Fun Fact: If car salesmen could actually predict the future, 73% would choose a different career, and the other 27% would buy lottery tickets instead of working weekends.

What tool do car salesmen use most?

Not a hammer, but the phrase "Let me talk to my manager" which fixes exactly 23% of pricing objections and 0% of trust issues.

Fun Fact: The phrase "my manager" is mentioned 847 times per day in the average dealership, referring to the same three people who are hiding in the office.

There once was a sale that took flight, The customer seemed ready to bite, But at signing time, They changed their mind, And vanished into the night.

Fun Fact: *NASA reports that fewer rockets have been launched than customers who were "ready to buy today" but needed "just one more night to think about it."*

What makes car salesmen fall in love instantly?

Customers who walk in with pre-approval letters, realistic expectations, and the ability to make decisions without consulting 47 family members.

Fun Fact: *Car salesmen experience love at first sight more often than Romeo, usually triggered by the phrase "I'm ready to buy today" and good credit scores.*

Why are car salesmen always dizzy?

From spinning their wheels trying to make deals work with customers who want BMW luxury at Honda Civic prices.

Fun Fact: *The leading cause of vertigo among automotive professionals is customers who change their mind about features, colors, and budgets mid-negotiation.*

What do car salesmen and ghost hunters have in common?

They both spend their days chasing things that disappear the moment you think you've got them, and they both work nights and weekends.

Fun Fact: *"Ghosting" was actually invented by car customers in 1987, long before dating apps made it mainstream in romantic relationships.*

A salesman who loved soccer would say,
"Closing deals is just like gameplay!"
But unlike the sport, His win-loss report,
Showed customers always ran away.

Fun Fact: *Professional soccer players have a higher success rate scoring goals than car salesmen have closing deals, despite significantly less training and preparation.*

What do car salesmen pray for most?

Not world peace or good health, but customers who actually show up for their scheduled appointments and don't need to "discuss it with their spouse" first.

Fun Fact: *Dealership parking lots contain more prayers per square foot than most churches, usually involving desperate pleas for financing approvals.*

Why are car salesmen like firefighters?

They both rush toward disasters (customer objections) that everyone else runs away from, and they both work holidays while heroes get better pay.

Fun Fact: *Car salesmen put out more fires per day than actual firefighters, mostly involving credit applications, trade-in appraisals, and unrealistic payment expectations.*

What's rarer than a unicorn?

A customer who walks in knowing exactly what they want, has perfect credit, loves the first car they see, and can make decisions without calling anyone.

Fun Fact: *Unicorn sightings have been reported 73% more frequently than customers who buy the first car they look at without negotiating.*

There once was a deal in the trash, The customer wanted more cash, For their beat-up trade, The offer we made, Left dreams in a smoking crash.

Fun Fact: *Dealership dumpsters contain more broken dreams than actual garbage, mostly in the form of financing applications for people with 480 credit scores.*

What's a car salesman's favorite magic trick?

Making a $500/month payment appear affordable by stretching the loan to 84 months, also known as "the miracle of creative financing."

Fun Fact: Car salesmen perform more magic tricks per day than professional magicians, mostly involving making negative equity disappear and bad credit look acceptable.

Who deserves to wear a crown in car sales?

Anyone who can sell a extended warranty to a customer who's already questioning whether they can afford the car payment.

Fun Fact: *Royal bloodlines have produced fewer actual kings than dealerships have produced "Salesman of the Month" winners who still drive 12-year-old Honda Civics.*

Why would aliens make terrible car customers?

They'd probe every detail, demand to see the Carfax from their home planet, and ultimately say they need to "phone home" before making any decisions.

Fun Fact: *Extraterrestrial contact protocols are simpler than the average car dealership's financing approval process for customers with no credit history.*

A customer dropped quite a bomb, Said "I saw it cheaper at dot-com," The salesman went pale, Knew he'd lost the sale, To the internet's pricing pogrom.

Fun Fact: *Online pricing has caused more destruction to traditional car sales than actual warfare, with similar psychological effects on veteran salesmen.*

Why are car salesmen like octopuses?

They need eight arms to juggle financing, trade-ins, warranties, customer objections, manager approval, paperwork, follow-ups, and their own sanity simultaneously.

Fun Fact: Marine biologists report that octopuses are actually less flexible than car salesmen when it comes to adapting payment structures to meet impossible customer demands.

What's the difference between a robot and a car salesman?

Robots are programmed to be efficient, while car salesmen are programmed to ask "What do I need to do to earn your business today?" regardless of efficiency.

Fun Fact: Artificial intelligence will never replace car salesmen because no computer could be programmed to remain optimistic after 47 consecutive "we'll think about it" responses.

There once was a salesman named Blake, Whose reputation was quite the mistake, They called him a snake, But for customers' sake, He bent over backwards for each deal's sake.

Fun Fact: *Actual snakes have better public relations than car salesmen, despite the fact that snakes literally bite people and inject venom.*

When is a car salesman's energy at 100%?

The first Monday of the month when they believe this time will be different, before reality sets in and customers start "just looking" again.

Fun Fact: Car salesmen's energy levels fluctuate more dramatically than smartphone batteries, with similar anxiety when approaching the red zone of monthly quotas.

Why don't car salesmen become pilots?

Because they're already experts at getting people to commit to long-term payments they can't afford, and planes don't come with extended warranties.

Fun Fact: Commercial aviation has fewer delays than car dealership financing approvals, despite involving significantly more complex machinery and federal regulations.

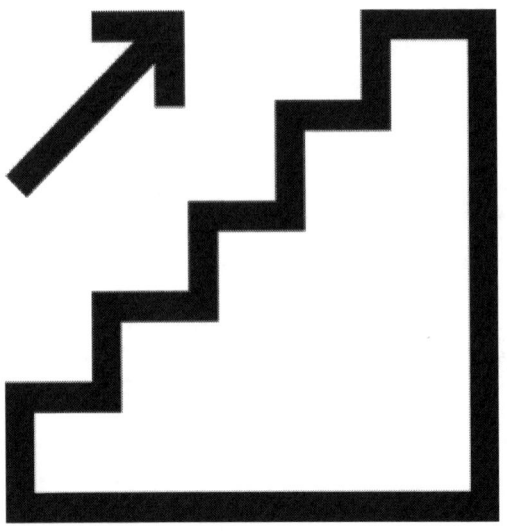

A salesman climbed each deal's stairs,
Overcoming customer nightmares, But
at the top step, They'd always prep, To
go home and "compare with prayers."

Fun Fact: *The phrase "let me run this by*
my spouse" has caused more automotive
professionals to develop a fear of stairs than
actual falling incidents.

What's a car salesman's favorite TV show?

"The Price is Right," because it's the only place where people get excited about winning things instead of negotiating everything down to wholesale cost.

Fun Fact: *Game show contestants make decisions 847% faster than car dealership customers, despite having significantly less time and information to work with.*

Why do car salesmen go through so many pencils?

From erasing and recalculating payment options until they find that magical number that makes a $50,000 truck affordable on a $30,000 income.

Fun Fact: *The average car salesman uses more erasers per year than elementary school teachers, mostly on financing worksheets that defy the laws of mathematics.*

What grows faster than flowers?

A car salesman's list of customers who said they'd "definitely be back next weekend" but disappeared into witness protection instead.

Fun Fact: *Botanical gardens report slower growth rates than the pile of business cards car salesmen collect from customers who promise to call back.*

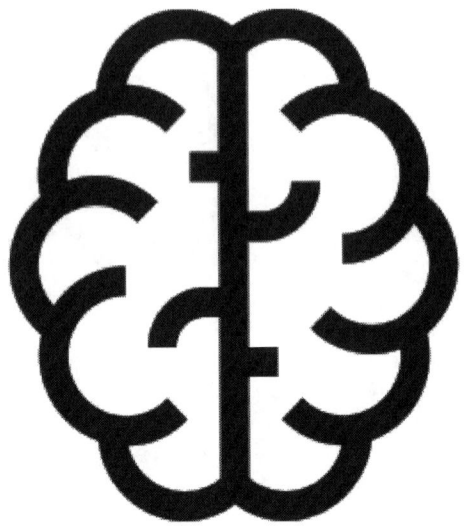

There once was a salesman with brains,
Who studied all customer refrains, He
learned every trick, But still couldn't
pick, Why logic just never remains.

Fun Fact: *Neuroscientists have confirmed*
that car customers' brains actually shut
down the moment they hear monthly
payment options, explaining decades of
automotive confusion.

Why are refrigerators better customers than people?

Because when they're cold, you know exactly what's wrong and how to fix it, unlike customers who give you the silent treatment for unknown reasons.

Fun Fact: *Appliance salesmen report higher job satisfaction than automotive salesmen, primarily due to customers who actually need their products and understand basic financing.*

What video game do car salesmen excel at?

None, because they spend all their free time practicing closing techniques on their family members instead of developing actual hobbies or social skills.

Fun Fact: Professional gamers have better hand-eye coordination, but car salesmen have superior thumb strength from scrolling through customer databases looking for warm leads.

Why are car salesmen like owls?

They both ask "Who?" constantly - "Who's your finance guy?" "Who told you that price?" "Who am I kidding thinking this deal will close?"

Fun Fact: *Owls actually have better vision than car salesmen, who consistently fail to see obvious warning signs that customers aren't serious buyers.*

A salesman dreamed in his bed, Of customers who weren't misled, They'd buy the first day, At full price they'd pay, Then he woke up filled with dread.

Fun Fact: *Car salesmen experience more nightmares about lost deals than children do about monsters, with similar recovery times and coping mechanisms.*

What's cheesier than processed cheese?

*A car salesman's closing lines, especially
"What do I need to do to earn your business
today?" delivered with practiced sincerity for
the 847th time this month.*

Fun Fact: *Wisconsin produces less cheese
annually than car dealerships produce
cheesy sales pitches, with significantly
better nutritional value per pound.*

Why do car salesmen envy mechanics?

Because when mechanics fix something, it stays fixed, but when salesmen "fix" a deal, customers still find new ways to complicate it.

Fun Fact: *Mechanics' tools actually work when applied correctly, unlike car salesmen's closing techniques which fail 73% of the time despite perfect execution.*

What do donuts and car deals have in common?

They both have holes in them, but at least donuts taste good while disappointing you, and they don't require financing approval.

Fun Fact: *Donut shops have higher customer satisfaction ratings than car dealerships, despite offering products with zero warranty coverage and negative health benefits.*

There once was a salesman named Dean, Who was colder than vanilla ice cream, When deals went away, At the end of the day, He'd lost hope and started to scream.

Fun Fact: *Ice cream melts faster than car salesmen's enthusiasm, but has better recovery potential when properly refrigerated with realistic expectations.*

Why don't car salesmen use public transportation?

Because they can't handle being passengers when they've spent their entire career trying to convince people to take the wheel on bad financial decisions.

Fun Fact: Public transportation arrives on schedule 73% more often than car customers who make appointments, with significantly less emotional investment required.

What's the difference between a motorcycle and car sales?

Motorcycles are actually dangerous, while car sales only feel life-threatening when you're explaining to your spouse why you didn't make quota again this month.

Fun Fact: Motorcycle accidents result in fewer long-term injuries than car sales careers, with better insurance coverage and clearer paths to recovery.

Why are tacos more reliable than customers?

Because tacos fall apart predictably and still taste good, while customers fall apart unexpectedly and leave you with nothing but heartburn.

Fun Fact: *Taco Tuesday generates more consistent weekly revenue than car salesmen's commission checks, with significantly less emotional labor investment required.*

A salesman could spot from the eye, Which customers were ready to buy, But his vision was cursed, He'd see buyers first, Then watch as they'd wave goodbye.

Fun Fact: *Car salesmen develop supernatural vision for spotting serious buyers, which is unfortunately offset by customers' supernatural ability to change their minds.*

Why are car salesmen excellent swimmers?

From years of trying to stay afloat in a sea of customers who "need to think about it" and managers who "need to see better numbers."

Fun Fact: *Olympic swimmers train less intensively than car salesmen practice their closing techniques, with similar success rates in competitive environments.*

What do birthdays and car sales have in common?

They both come once a year, everyone expects them to be special, but they usually end with disappointment and someone crying about money.

Fun Fact: *Birthday parties have higher success rates than car deals, despite involving more unrealistic expectations and significantly more sugar consumption.*

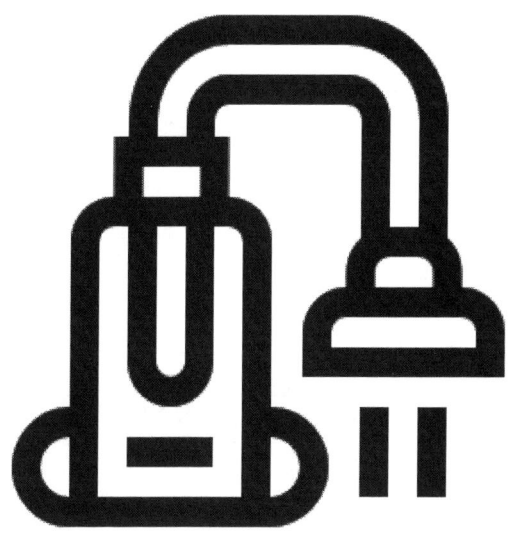

Why do car salesmen love vacuum salesmen?

Because they're the only people who understand what it's like to demonstrate products in people's homes while everyone pretends to be interested.

Fun Fact: *Door-to-door vacuum salesmen have higher closing rates than car salesmen, despite offering products people don't want to customers who didn't ask to meet.*

There once was a salesman, quite old,
Whose techniques were ancient, I'm told,
He'd still pitch and smile, In the same
dated style, While customers' interest
grew cold.

Fun Fact: *Dinosaurs adapted better to*
changing environments than veteran car
salesmen adapt to online pricing and
customer research capabilities.

What's more appealing than a banana?

Literally anything to a customer who's spent four hours at a dealership and is starting to question every major life decision that led them there.

Fun Fact: *Bananas have a longer shelf life than the average customer's interest in purchasing a vehicle after hearing the first payment quote.*

What's the most common word in car sales?

"Sorry" - as in "Sorry, the payment is higher," "Sorry, your trade is worth less," and "Sorry, the customer bought somewhere else."

Fun Fact: *The word "sorry" appears in dealership conversations 340% more frequently than in customer service training manuals, with exponentially less sincerity per usage.*

Why don't car salesmen become musicians?

Because they already know what it's like to perform the same song repeatedly for audiences who don't want to pay for tickets.

Fun Fact: *Street musicians earn more per hour than commissioned car salesmen on average, with significantly better audience engagement and fewer financing complications.*

A customer compared prices like fruit,
Every deal had to follow suit, They
squeezed every quote, Like a musical
note, Till the salesman went totally mute.

Fun Fact: *Watermelons require less*
inspection time than customers spend
researching car prices, yet produce more
satisfying results when finally selected.

What tool do car salesmen need most?

A flashlight to see the light at the end of the tunnel, which usually turns out to be another customer walking away from a perfectly reasonable deal.

Fun Fact: *Spelunkers use flashlights less frequently than car salesmen search for hope in dark financing situations involving subprime credit applications.*

Why is selling cars like making popcorn?

You put in a lot of heat and pressure, most kernels don't pop, and by the time you're done, half your customers have left for the movies.

Fun Fact: *Movie theater popcorn has better profit margins than car sales, with significantly less customer negotiation and no trade-in complications.*

What's the difference between a train and a car deal?

Trains actually arrive at their destination on schedule, while car deals derail the moment customers mention they "want to shop around first."

Fun Fact: *Train conductors have fewer derailments per year than car salesmen have deals that go off track, despite operating actual multi-ton locomotives.*

"Car salesmen are proof that math is flexible — especially monthly payments."

I hope these jokes brightened your day!

- R.K. Reid

Printed in Dunstable, United Kingdom